VIEWPOINTS AND PERSPECTIVES

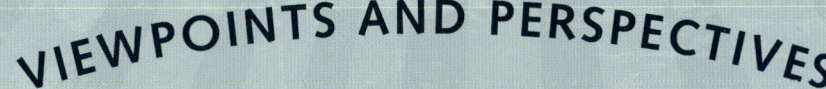

VIEWPOINTS ON THE OREGON TRAIL AND WESTWARD EXPANSION

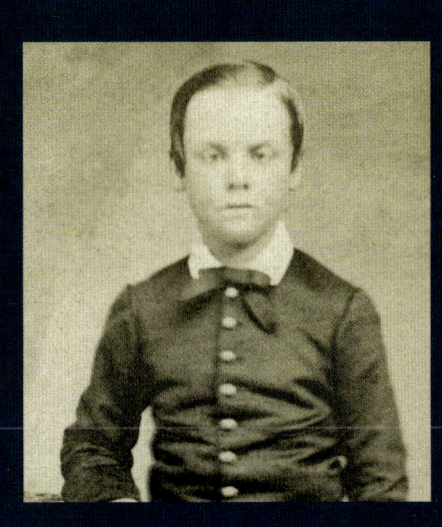

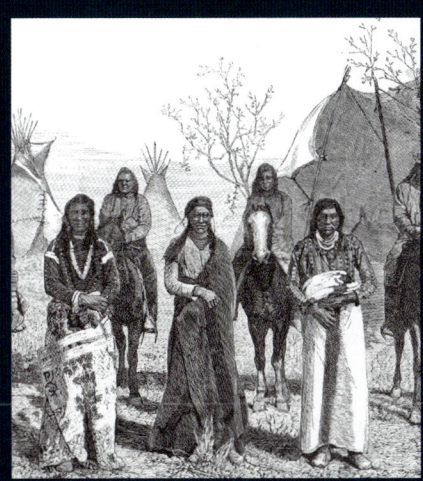

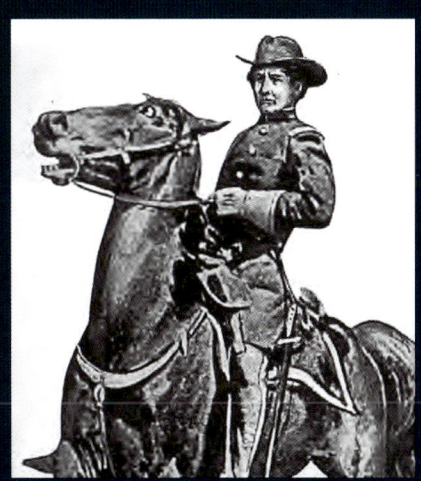

PART OF THE PERSPECTIVES LIBRARY

KRISTIN J. RUSSO

Published in the United States of America by Cherry Lake Publishing
Ann Arbor, Michigan
www.cherrylakepublishing.com

Reading Adviser: Marla Conn MS, Ed., Literacy specialist, Read-Ability, Inc.

Photo Credits: ©Donna Beeler/Shutterstock, cover (left); ©Everett Collection/Newscom, cover (middle); ©Wikimedia, cover (right); ©Donna Beeler/Shutterstock, 1 (left); ©Everett Collection/Newscom, 1 (middle); ©Wikimedia, 1 (right); ©Donna Beeler/Shutterstock, 4; ©bauhaus1000/Getty Images, 7; ©bauhaus1000/Getty Images, 9; ©bauhaus1000/Getty Images, 10; ©bauhaus1000/Getty Images, 13; ©bauhaus1000/Getty Images, 14; ©Everett Collection/Newscom, 18; ©duncan1890/Getty Images, 19; ©ZUMAPRESS.com/Newscom, 21; ©Quint Lox/Newscom, 25; ©Wikimedia, 26; ©Grafissimo/Getty Images, 31; ©Wikimedia, 32; ©bauhaus1000/Getty Images, 35; ©Wikimedia, 36; ©Album/Prisma/Newscom, 39; ©Album/Prisma/Newscom, 41; ©ivanastar/Getty Images, 44; ©raclro/Getty Images, 45; ©LondonStarDesigns/Getty Images, 45; ©Quint Lox/Newscom, 46

Copyright ©2019 by Cherry Lake Publishing
All rights reserved. No part of this book may be reproduced or utilized in
any form or by any means without written permission from the publisher.

Library of Congress Cataloging-in-Publication Data has been filed and is available at catalog.loc.gov

Cherry Lake Publishing would like to acknowledge the work of The Partnership for 21st Century Learning.
Please visit *www.p21.org* for more information.

Printed in the United States of America
Corporate Graphics

TABLE OF CONTENTS

In this book, you will read about the Oregon Trail and westward expansion from three perspectives. Each perspective is based on real things that happened to real people who traveled or experienced the Oregon Trail. As you'll see, the same event can look different depending on one's point of view.

CHAPTER 1 4
Jesse A. Applegate: Traveler on the Oregon Trail

CHAPTER 2 18
Otter Woman: Shoshone Woman, Friend to Sacagawea

CHAPTER 3 32
General Stephen Watts Kearny: "The Father of the United States Cavalry"

TIMELINE 44

LOOK, LOOK AGAIN 46

GLOSSARY 47

LEARN MORE 47

INDEX 48

ABOUT THE AUTHOR 48

JESSE A. APPLEGATE

Traveler on the Oregon Trail

My name is Jesse Applegate Applegate. My parents named me that so that people won't confuse me with my uncle, whose name is just Jesse Applegate. Some folks call me Jesse A. Others just call me Jess. My family and I are headed west to Oregon, "to collect our riches," Pa says. My ma and pa, uncles and aunts, brothers and cousins are all going on the trip. Our whole family is moving out west together.

Up 'til now, we've been farming right here in Missouri. I like it here, but Pa says it is hard to make a living as a farmer in Missouri. Too many other farmers are crowding us in, and we've got mosquitoes and diseases to worry us now, too. Pa says we either go west or wait around here to catch malaria or yellow fever. Oregon is the "land of milk and honey," he says.

> **THINK ABOUT IT**
> Read this paragraph closely. What is its main point? Cite specific evidence from the text to support your answer.

Of course, there's no going against Pa. He says we're leaving and that is that. Since about 1811, it's been mostly fur trappers and traders making their way past the Mississippi River. Pa says now that it's 1843, the trappers, traders, missionaries, and other explorers have been coming and going back and forth long enough to prove it can be done. So we loaded

> **SECOND SOURCE**
>
> Find an outside source that describes life along the Oregon Trail. Compare the information from your source to the information here. How are they alike? How are they different?

our wagon with everything we own and joined a big group of other folks headed in the same direction. "There's safety in numbers," says Pa, though he didn't say what kind of danger he expected to meet. We set off from Independence, Missouri, in May with nearly 1,000 other folks. We are in what is called a "**wagon train**." The "train" is not really a train. It's a line of wagons. Ours has hundreds of wagons, oxen, and cattle all in a line as far as the eye can see.

Pa said we had to choose the time of our leaving carefully. If we left too early in the spring, there would be no grass yet for the livestock once we reached the plains. If we left too late, we might get caught in winter storms in the mountains. Pa seems awful sure about this. I've got no choice but to go along and trust him.

THOUSANDS OF WAGONS MAKING THEIR WAY ALONG THE OREGON TRAIL WORE RUTS INTO THE EARTH. MANY RUTS ARE STILL VISIBLE TODAY.

Here is a typical day on the wagon train:
Sentinels wake the camp with rifle fire at 4 o'clock in the morning. The early morning hours are the busiest. Between 5 and 7 o'clock, our camp is bustling with families cooking, eating, and cleaning up after breakfast. They yoke their grazing animals and vie for a good spot in line. Sometimes, fights break out over which family belongs where in the "train." By 7 o'clock,

MANIFEST DESTINY

"Manifest destiny" was the term politicians and leaders used to explain why the United States was meant to spread across the entire North American continent. It meant the country was destined to expand to the West. John O'Sullivan first used the phrase in July 1845 in an article published in the *United States Magazine and Democratic Review*.

IF TRAVELERS DID NOT REACH WYOMING BY JULY 4, IT WAS UNLIKELY THAT THEY WOULD REACH THEIR FINAL DESTINATION BEFORE WINTER.

a sentinel sounds his bugle, and we're off.

We stop at noontime to eat. This gives the oxen a chance to graze and rest. I'm too young to watch, but Pa says sometimes officers even hold court and try a person for committing a crime, like stealing or damaging someone else's property. No matter what,

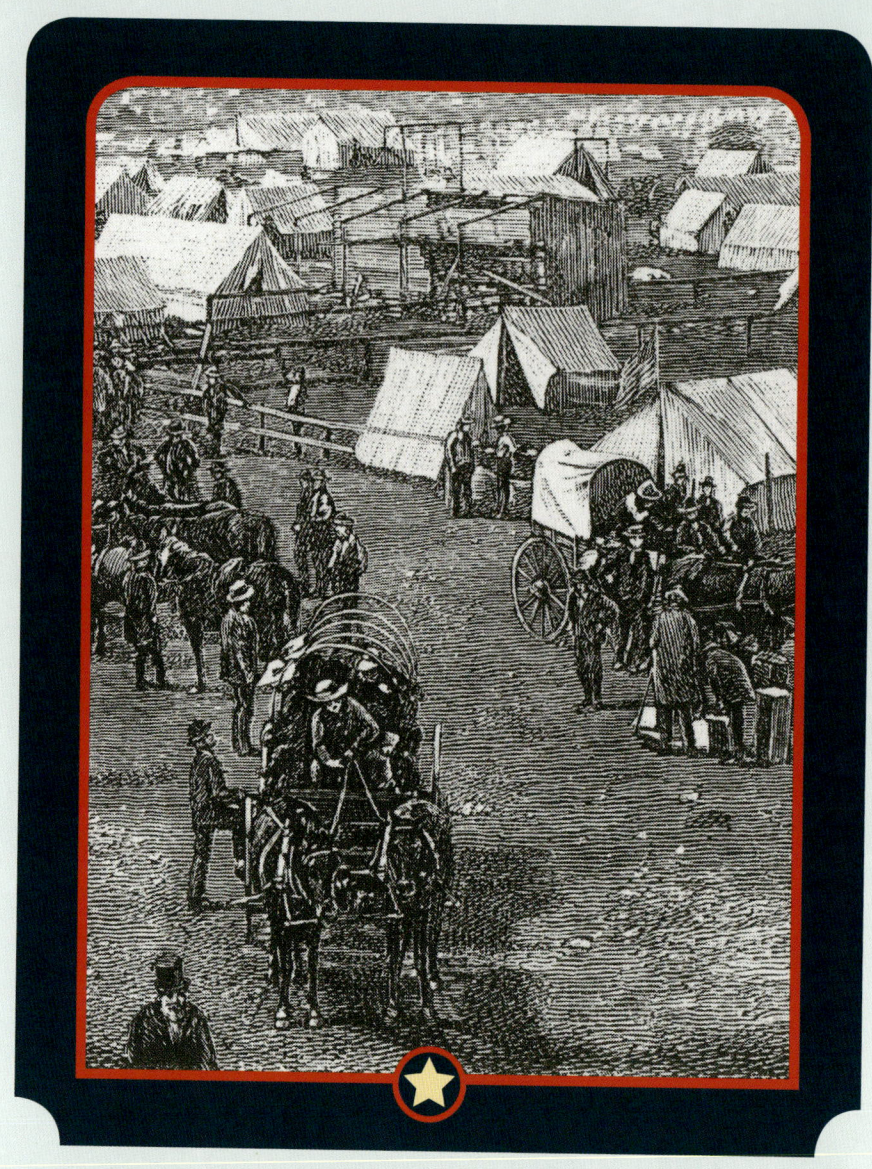

More than 400,000 people traveled the Oregon Trail between 1840 and 1880. Only about one in ten people died during the journey.

we are on our way again at 1 o'clock in the afternoon, and we travel nonstop until the leader finds a good spot to stop for the night. That is when the real fun starts. All the families make dinner and we all feast. Then it is time for the children to play and for the adults to sit around and talk. Sometimes, someone will play the fiddle and there will be dancing.

At 8 o'clock at night, guard duty starts. Various men take watch duty throughout the night. Pa says they're just watching the fire dim and keeping an eye out for wild animals, but I have a feeling they're watching for Native Americans, too. We have not had any trouble with the Native Americans we have come across. In fact, we played with some Native American children and traded nails and small bits of metal with them. We could not understand their language and they could not understand ours, but we still had fun! The adults are suspicious of the Native Americans, though, and it makes me afraid.

Our wagon is filled with sacks of flour and furniture and clothes and the like, so we do most of our cooking and eating and even sleeping outside under the great big sky. Pa says our journey is more than 2,000 miles (3,200 kilometers). The journey is pretty slow going. The oxen are strong, but they are pulling a heavy load, and when their hooves split, you can see that they are in pain.

We've been on the road some months now, and many of the animals that pull the wagons are getting tired. The wagons are heavy, and they cannot go on. We have to wait until families **discard** some of their heavier items, like stoves and tables and chairs. I do not know why anyone would even haul a stove across the **prairie**, but Pa says that where we are going, there are no stores to buy the things we need. If folks want a stove, they have to bring it with them. But Pa gets impatient when another family holds us up.

Our wagon has a waterproof covering, but luckily

we've had mostly good weather so far. It is good that we haven't had to climb in the back with all the gear. It's suffocating back there. Bowed hickory holds the canvas cover in place and iron wheels with wooden rims keep us on the move. Pa was furious when one of the wooden

THE "BED" OF A WAGON WAS A BOX ABOUT 4 FEET (1.2 METERS) WIDE BY 10 FEET (3 METERS) LONG.

IF A WAGON FELL OFF INTO A RAVINE, IT HAD TO BE LIGHT ENOUGH FOR PEOPLE AND ANIMALS TO PULL IT BACK OUT.

rims shrank and the iron tire slipped out. He kept muttering "wasting time, wasting time" as he reassembled the wheel. We have extra parts with us, because there is nowhere to buy replacements on the way.

We also have to carry all of our own food. Pa was warned that each family would need more than 1,000 pounds (450 kilograms) of food to keep us fed on the journey. That means our wagon is filled with flour and sugar, coffee and salt, and even about 150 pounds (70 kg) of bacon!

Sometimes, there are terrible thunderstorms that sweep across the plains. When this happens, I do not mind at all scurrying into the back of the wagon. The sky roars and the rain falls like bullets. Under cover is the best place to be!

After five months moving slowly on the wagon train, Pa says our 2,200-mile (3,540-km) journey is almost at an end. We are on the last leg. Unfortunately, for much of this leg, we must travel along the rivers. Pa and my uncles built boats for us when we stopped at **Fort Walla Walla**. These boats are meant to take us the rest of the way down the Columbia River.

Oh, how it grieves me to tell you this part of our journey. As our boat floated down the Columbia, it picked up speed. We headed straight toward the rapids, and we had no way to stop! I was with my parents, Elisha, Uncle Jesse, Aunt Cynthia, and a Native American whose name I did not know. He was our guide. In another boat were my brother Warren, my cousin Edward, two other men whom I did not know well, and a 70-year-old man named Alexander McClellan. Mr. McClellan was an army veteran and was fit as a fiddle considering his age, but even he was no match for these turbulent waters!

As we approached the river bend, I heard my aunt and my mother cry out! The skiff holding my brother and cousin had capsized! Warren went under, and we could not see him at all! He never came back up for a breath!

Mr. McClellan did his best to save Edward. He held two oars to which Edward clung with all his might. Mr. McClellan tried to swim to shore while holding on to the oars, but soon he was swept under the water. My cousin was lost, too. Mr. McClellan could have saved himself by letting go of Edward earlier. He is a hero for trying to hang on for so long.

I am heartbroken. My mother and aunt are inconsolable, and yet we must go on. We have no choice. We have come too far to turn back.

2

OTTER WOMAN
SHOSHONE WOMAN, FRIEND TO SACAGAWEA

Do the *newi* have trouble with the white man? Well, I guess that depends on whom you ask.

I think we have always had some level of trouble. Years ago, my friend Sacagawea and I were both taken captive from our Shoshone homes and brought to live in another Native American village. We were terribly homesick at first, but most people get used to a new way of life when they have to, and that is what Sacagawea and I did. It was a comfort to be with my friend. We shared a home in the village, and it helped

MANY SHOSHONE NATIVE AMERICANS WERE FUR TRADERS FROM ABOUT 1825 TO 1845. MANY SHOSHONE PEOPLE TODAY ARE RANCHERS AND FARMERS.

to ease our homesickness to have one another. We tried to speak to each other in our native languages, which are similar. It was a comfort to hear words close to my own mother tongue.

When Sacagawea left the village to go on a long journey with her French husband and two other white men named Meriwether Lewis and William Clark, I missed her very much. I have not seen my friend in a long time. I have seen much happiness and sadness through the years as white settlers make their way across the plains in covered wagons.

In the early days, during the times of Chief Cameahwait, who was Sacagawea's brother, there were mostly fair dealings between the Native American nations and the white men and women. I have seen our own Shoshone help the white settlers who were lost or in trouble. Shoshone people served as guides and helped to round up the white men's cattle when they got loose on the prairie. We would trade with the white

SACAGAWEA GAVE BIRTH TO HER FIRST SON, JEAN BAPTISTE CHARBONNEAU, WHILE SHE TRAVELED WITH HER HUSBAND ON THE LEWIS AND CLARK EXPEDITION.

travelers, too—hatchets and cookware and clothing for fresh meat and animal hides. Things were peaceful in the old days, but now times have changed. We hardly ever have peace. This is not the Shoshone way, and it is not our doing.

The new Shoshone Chief—Tonaioza, which means "buffalo robe"—is angered by the white travelers. He says people in the covered wagons let their own cattle graze on our lands and chase away our wild buffalo. The white people do not like Tonaioza. They call him Chief Pocatello. Pocatello is not even a Shoshone word. They mixed our language with theirs and gave him a name that means "he does not follow the road." The white men and women call other Shoshone "the snake people." This could be because other Native American groups use a hand gesture that looks like a snake when they refer to us. Or it could be because we live close to Snake River. I am not sure. I think it might be an insult. We are *newi*—regular people.

Mostly Shoshone still try to deal fairly with the white travelers. We continue to trade with them and help them when they are in trouble. But other Native American nations attack their wagon trains and steal from them. This makes the white travelers suspicious of all Native American nations, and they are beginning to attack us for insults and provocations that are not the fault of the Shoshone people.

Tonaioza was respected by all in our community, even when he was a young man. Many *newi* turned to him for advice about simple matters. This is still the way, though our problems are more complicated now. *Newi* ask Tonaioza what to do about the white travelers who steal food and attack our people. Tonaioza has advised them to fight back. Now, he and other Shoshone warriors have begun to challenge the wagon trains, demanding food to replace what the white people have used or chased away. Some white people give them what they want to avoid further

> **ANALYZE THIS**
>
> Compare the experiences of the pioneers moving west to those of the Native Americans. How are their experiences similar? How are they different?

trouble, but others do not. The white people have complained to their leaders about us. They say that we harass them during their travels, but we only want what is fair. The leaders of the white travelers have threatened us with war.

In 1859, two Shoshone men were killed by white men, though they had done nothing to deserve this. Tonaioza sent warriors to retaliate, and they killed six white travelers. Tonaioza was captured, but he was later released. The white leaders did not believe that Tonaioza was responsible for the death of the travelers. This made Tonaioza bold, and he continued to demand that the white travelers return what they were taking from the Shoshone people— our land and our source of food.

In the summer of 1862, Tonaioza and a party of warriors charged against a wagon train as it travelled

IN 1869, A FERRY WAS ESTABLISHED TO CARRY PIONEERS ACROSS SNAKE RIVER. BEFORE THE FERRY EXISTED, MANY PEOPLE DIED TRYING TO CROSS IN THEIR WAGONS OR MAKESHIFT RAFTS.

through the City of Rocks, in Idaho. A few days later, they attacked two other wagon trains near Snake River. Many white men were killed in these skirmishes, but what did the white travelers expect? That they could continue to travel over our lands and

On January 29, 1863, Colonel Patrick Connor led an attack on Shoshone Native Americans who were camped at a bend in Bear River in what is now Idaho. This event is known as the Bear River Massacre.

to disrupt our way of life without giving back? We can only take so much. We also need land on which to live and food to eat. It is the Shoshone warrior's duty to provide for his people. Surely the white travelers can understand this. They provide for their own families just as we do.

    Tonaioza's decision to embark on these attacks cost us all dearly in the end. The white travelers sent for a stronger leader to help them. Soon, Colonel Patrick Connor arrived at Camp Douglas near Salt Lake City. He planned an attack on the Shoshone people, which he carried out in the winter of 1863. More than 350 Shoshone—men, women, and children—were killed by Connor and his soldiers when they attacked their camp near Bear River. The Shoshone people were not prepared for this attack and could not defend themselves. Colonel Connor lost only 22 of his own soldiers in the skirmish. We describe this event with an English word. We call it a massacre.

But Colonel Connor was not finished. Once the survivors of the Bear River Massacre signed a peace treaty promising to leave all white travelers alone, Connor and his soldiers searched the countryside for all the Shoshone men and women who had run away to escape the attack. He mostly wanted to find Tonaioza. Connor planned to kill our leader to weaken our people.

Tonaioza avoided capture for a long time, but he finally decided that if he gave himself up, Colonel Connor and his soldiers would stop killing other Shoshone. He turned himself in. Instead of killing Tonaioza, they forced him and eight other Native American nation chiefs to sign a treaty agreeing to leave white travelers alone. In this agreement, called the Treaty of Box Elder, Tonaioza also agreed to give up two-thirds of Shoshone hunting grounds so that the white travelers could have it. All we have left now is the land between Raft River and the Portneuf Mountains. We are afraid that this will not yield enough food or animal hides for all of us to eat and to stay warm. I think the white leaders know this too, because they offered to give us money each year to buy food and blankets.

The money does not come, though. If it does, it

TREATIES

Treaties between the United States and Native Americans resulted in the United States taking more and more land away from the Native Americans. Just nine years before the Treaty of Box Elder, the Kansas-Nebraska Act of 1854 took land from Indian territory to create the states of Kansas and Nebraska.

comes too late, and our people suffer. We need to buy food if we are not allowed to hunt it. The white leaders have not kept the promise they made in the treaty. And so Tonaioza has begun to lead raids on wagon trains and to steal from white men and women traveling in stagecoaches that now carry travelers out west. They are careful not to hurt the travelers if they can help it, and steal only food because we are starving. We also beg for food, which is humiliating.

> **SECOND SOURCE**
> What is the main point of this chapter? Identify two pieces of evidence that support this idea.

I do not hold out hope that we will have good, peaceful relationships with the white men and women and their leaders. From what I can see, they take what they want, no matter whom it belongs to, and they do not keep their promises. The *newi* have always had trouble with the white invaders, and I fear that we always will.

Most Native American groups, including the Shoshone, tolerated and even helped pioneers along the Oregon Trail.

3

GENERAL STEPHEN WATTS KEARNY

"THE FATHER OF THE UNITED STATES CAVALRY"

They will not make it. I can tell by the look of them. As an old soldier who has seen too many battles, I have experience in these matters. I can tell when a person cannot go another step without help. Of course, I will do what I can for them. I'm talking about the party that Stephen Meek is leading, of course. This is the longest wagon train by far that I have ever seen—

well more than 400 wagons by my estimate. That many wagons could be carrying up to 3,000 people. I ride ahead and speak to Meek. I discuss his plans with him, and it seems he may have overestimated his ability to bring this many people across. I can only imagine that he thought the road to the West would be clear and long-enough established to take this many people across. He was wrong. These people are suffering.

Life on the Oregon Trail is hard under the best of circumstances. Since 1842, I have been charged with providing safe passage for emigrants making their way out west. As we travel from fort to fort to keep watch, we soldiers see what it does to people. The rivers alone are among the biggest threats. Swollen rivers tip over wagons and makeshift rafts drown folks. Those waters are no friend to the oxen, either. Many a beast has met his demise in the cold and furious rapids. Or they could just plain panic while they are wading through the deep water, losing valuable property at best or killing their passengers at worst! Some folks are even crushed by wagons or wagon wheels, or else thrown by their horses.

If they are not carried off by the swollen rivers or crushed by unruly animals, they face the risk of getting run over by their own wagons. Snake bites, stampeding livestock, accidental firearm discharges, and all manner of diseases account for even more misery. Once **cholera** or **small pox** takes hold of a group of travelers, it spreads quickly through the entire camp. They tell me if the end is near for one soul, they will wait to give the person a peaceful passing.

Burial is a hardship, though, without caskets. Many folks were buried in as deep a grave as their people could dig. They are buried right in the middle of the trail so wagons roll over the grave and animals trample it down. This erases the scent of the dead, you

PIONEERS CAUGHT IN SNOW STORMS OFTEN SUFFERED FROSTBITE OR EVEN FROZE TO DEATH.

see, keeping the wolves and other wild, scavenging animals at bay.

They've begun to keep records of the emigration. According to the numbers, only one in ten people who

Stephen Meek led about 200 wagons away from an established path on the Oregon Trail. As a result, the group struggled to find water and 23 people died.

set off on the Oregon Trail make it to the end. Those are some scary odds. But I understand the need to provide the best for one's family, both in material goods and in opportunity. My wife, Mary, is William Clark's stepdaughter. An adventurous spirit and a yearning for a better life is more than just family tradition, it is human nature. It is my job to help others reach their destinations, wherever they may lead.

    I ride awhile with Meek to discover his plans and he tells me something alarming. He plans to leave the trail. He is certain he can find a shortcut to California. Those that want to go on to Oregon as planned will be free to do so, but he thinks he can guide the rest south to California on a route never taken before. I believe this is **hubris**, and he will be sorry, but I cannot command him to abandon his plans. I can only do what I can to ensure the safe passage of as many of these people as possible.

Before I leave the group, I check in with a few others. Sure enough, they have their heart set on splitting up the group. A young man named Samuel Hancock says he has faith in Meek. Says Meek knows a shortcut to California, one that's packed down and easy to travel.

Whether they stay together or split up, this many people are an easy target for disgruntled Native American groups who will not welcome what will appear to be a vast invasion of their hunting grounds. I will have to do something to try to head off trouble.

Having discovered what I can about Meek's group and their plans, I ride ahead with my soldiers to organize a meeting with Plains Native American group leaders. Quickly, my party and I make our way to Fort Laramie. From here,

> **SECOND SOURCE**
> Find another source about Fort Laramie or other forts along the Oregon Trail. Compare the information from that source to the information in this chapter. How is it similar? How is it different?

In 1851, an important treaty was reached at Fort Laramie with the Plains Native American groups. The treaty defined borders between their lands.

we organize a meeting with Native Americans and their leaders to work out an agreement that will ensure the emigrants' safe passage. About 1,200 Sioux Native

END OF THE TRAIL

The Oregon Trail was heavily traveled until 1884, when Union Pacific completed a railroad along the same route. After that, it was much faster and less expensive to travel to the West by rail. The trail was still used to move cattle for many years.

FORT LARAMIE PROVIDED A PLACE FOR PIONEERS TO REST AND REPLENISH SUPPLIES ALONG THE OREGON TRAIL.

Americans attend this council, which takes place near Fort Laramie.

Fort Laramie is located in a most convenient place for both travelers and the military. Traveling folks have come to look for it and welcome the respite and food it provides. The fort started as a place for trading where the North Platte and Laramie rivers met. Its name back then was Fort William. Now that it is a U.S. military fort, it has been renamed for Jacques La Ramie, a French fur trapper.

We do important work here. Though there has not been too much trouble between the American travelers and the Native American groups that live on the plains, conflicts are becoming more common. It is our job to sort these problems out, with diplomacy if possible, with gunfire if not. Sometimes, I leave that decision up to my cavalrymen. Often, I'll order my soldiers to accompany and guard wagon trains against Native American attacks, but Meek's group is too large.

Thankfully, our meeting just outside Fort Laramie is productive. We are able to negotiate a peace treaty with the Native American groups. We reach an agreement, and the Sioux and other Native American groups will allow this and other wagon trains to make their way safely across the plains. This is an enormous relief to me. I consider my post to secure the safe passage of U.S. citizens across the prairies and plains toward the West a difficult but solemn duty.

> **ANALYZE THIS**
>
> Think about the viewpoint of the soldier at Fort Laramie. How are his views similar to the settlers and the Native Americans? How are they different?

TIMELINE
THE OREGON TRAIL

1820
The western fur trading industry is under way.

1827
Independence, Missouri, becomes a city. Later, it is established as the starting point for pioneers beginning their travels on the Oregon Trail.

1841
Pioneers begin to travel west in wagon trains on the Oregon Trail.

Nearly 1,000 people travel the Oregon Trail. This is called the "Great Emigration."

1843

The United States government formally recognizes the Oregon Territory as an official territory.

1848

The trail is recognized by the U.S. Congress and officially named the Oregon National Historic Trail. Very little of the original trail still exists, but about 300 miles (480 km) of it has been preserved. Visitors can still see ruts made from old wagon wheels.

1978

Look, Look Again

Take a close look at this photograph of Snake River and answer the following questions:

1. What would a young boy traveling west see in this picture? What would he think of the dangers he would face crossing such a river?

2. What would a Native American see in this picture? Would they consider this area part of their home? How would a Native American feel about newcomers traveling along a river and into areas that Native Americans had always considered their own lands?

3. What would pioneers think about this scene? Would they think about the safest, easiest ways to cross such a river? Would they consider the possibility that they were trespassing on Native American land? Or would they be concerned mostly with traveling and crossing the river safely?

GLOSSARY

cavalry *(CAH-vahl-ree)* soldiers who fought on horseback

cholera *(KAWL-ur-ah)* an often fatal disease people get from drinking from an infected water supply

discard *(dis-KARD)* to throw away; to get rid of

Fort Walla Walla *(FORT WAHLA WAHLA)* located in the state of Washington, this fort provided a place for pioneers traveling on the Oregon Trail to stop for protection and supplies

hubris *(HYOO-bris)* excessive pride or self-confidence

prairie *(PRAH-ree)* a large open area of grassland

sentinels *(SEN-ten-elz)* guards

Shoshone *(shuh-SHO-nee or shuh-SHONE)* a group of Native Americans that lived in areas of what is now California, Nevada, Utah, Idaho, and Wyoming

small pox *(SMOL POCKS)* an often fatal disease caused by a virus

wagon train *(wah-GONE TRANE)* a column of wagons traveling together from east to west on the Oregon Trail

LEARN MORE

FURTHER READING

Gibson, Karen Bush. *The Oregon Trail: The Journey Across the Country from Lewis and Clark to the Transcontinental Railroad.* White River Junction, VT: Nomad Press, 2017.

Gregory, Josh. *If You Were a Kid on the Oregon Trail.* New York: Children's Press, 2017.

Messner, Kate. *Rescue on the Oregon Trail.* New York: Scholastic Press, 2015.

WEBSITES

Oregon National Historic Trail
https://www.nps.gov/oreg/index.htm
Read about the people and places of the Oregon National Historic Trail.

Oregon Trail: Facts and Summary
http://www.history.com/topics/oregon-trail
Learn important facts about the history of the Oregon Trail.

INDEX

cholera, 34
Clark, William, 20, 21, 37
Connor, Colonel Patrick, 26, 27, 28

Fort Laramie, 29, 38, 39, 40, 41, 42, 43
Fort Walla Walla, 15

Lewis, Meriwether, 20, 21

Manifest Destiny, 8
Meek, Stephen, 32, 33, 36, 37, 38, 42
Mississippi River, 5

Native Americans, 11, 16, 18, 19, 20, 22, 23, 24, 26, 28, 29, 31, 38, 39, 40, 42, 43, 46

oxen, 6, 9, 12, 33

Sacagawea, 18, 19, 20, 21
small pox, 34
Snake River, 22, 25, 46

Tonaioza, 22, 23, 24, 27, 28, 30
treaties, 28, 29, 30, 39, 43

wagons, 6, 7, 12, 13, 14, 15, 20, 22, 23, 24, 25, 30, 32, 33, 34, 36, 42, 43, 44, 45

ABOUT THE AUTHOR

Kristin J. Russo is a university English lecturer. She loves teaching, reading, writing, and learning new things. She and her husband live near Providence, Rhode Island, in a small house surrounded by flower gardens. They have three grown children and three rescue dogs.